Swimming

Produced in collaboration with
the Amateur Swimming Association

Produced for A & C Black by
Monkey Puzzle Media Ltd
Gissings Farm, Fressingfield
Suffolk IP21 5SH

Published in 2006 by
A & C Black Publishers Ltd
38 Soho Square, London W1D 3HB
www.acblack.com

Fourth edition 2006

ISBN-10: 0 7136 7701 5
ISBN-13: 978 0 7136 7701 0

A CIP record for this book is available from the
British Library.

Acknowledgements
Cover and inside design by James Winrow for
Monkey Puzzle Media Ltd.
Cover photograph courtesy of Empics. Photographs on
pages 4, 25, 31, 45, 51, 53 and 57 courtesy of SWPix.
All other photographs courtesy of Empics.

KNOW THE GAME is a registered trademark.

Printed and bound in China by C&C Offset Printing Co., Ltd.

CONTENTS

FOREWORD

Swimming is a sport for people of all ages and abilities, for both exercise and enjoyment. Being able to swim means children and adults alike are safer near water, and is essential if you want to participate in exciting water-based activities such as surfing or sailing.

One or two of these young racers may have started on the road to Olympic glory.

This book, written by the Amateur Swimming Association, sets out clearly the skills and knowledge required at each stage of learning how to swim, from developing initial water confidence to performing the main strokes and learning how to dive. It includes useful advice on helping even very young children feel at home in the water, so that they come to the swimming pool ready to enjoy developing their swimming skills.

In addition, this book offers sound advice to those who can already swim, but would like to improve their swimming skills.

SWIMMING AT SCHOOL

Swimming is an important part of the National Curriculum for Physical Education, particularly up to the age of 11 years. By the time children leave primary school – at the end of Key Stage 2 – they should be able to swim at least 25m and demonstrate an understanding of water safety. This book provides a framework for children to learn these skills and more.

Even the elite swimmers had to start with the basics of learning to swim.

BEGINNING TO SWIM

Early training

From the earliest days, bath-time provides babies with the experience of immersion. With the help of their parents they can enjoy splashing, kicking and floating. Things to think about include:

- no irritants in the water

- the water temperature should be comfortable

- the emphasis should be on fun.

As babies grow and are able to use the family bath, they will make movements on their front and on their back with support. Lots of babies enjoy blowing bubbles in the water, moving around while playing with familiar toys, and retrieving submerged objects. Gradually they discover the buoyancy that water offers – an important first step in beginning to swim.

NEVER leave young children unattended in the bath.

Early swimming pool experience

Because of the chlorine/ozone content in modern swimming pools, it is unlikely that infections such as polio and tetanus would be transmitted. Therefore, the immunisation status of a baby is not a major factor when considering the age at which a baby can swim. The suggested age for taking a baby to an adequately heated and maintained public pool is four to six months.

Getting started

To make sure their children enjoy their first visit to the pool, parents should provide the child with plenty of help. If the child is too small to reach the bottom of the pool, well-fitting buoyancy aids can be useful, plus gentle support from an adult.

FIRST IMPRESSIONS

A happy first experience is the key to future success and enjoyment of swimming. Warm, shallow water and relatively quiet conditions are best for learning. For younger children, the size, unfamiliar noise and crowds can make the swimming pool a bit overwhelming at first: a 'dry' visit to the pool can be a good way of getting children used to the idea.

▼ Parent-and-baby swimming classes are a great way to introduce children to the water.

This gives children the confidence to make exploratory movements in the water. Some children will adopt a horizontal position, while others will be more upright. From either position the child can be encouraged to make simple kicking movements of the legs and pulling movements of the arms, thus experiencing a feeling of propulsion.

Since children learn by imitation, showing children how the parents use their limbs to kick and pull is a good idea. If necessary, parents can help their children to learn the correct movements by holding their arms or legs and guiding them through the water. Repetition of these movements, accompanied by constant praise and encouragement, will accelerate learning. At this stage it is easier if all limb movements are made under the water. During these activities children should breathe naturally, but should be gradually introduced to the idea of breathing out into the water.

Confidence and learning ability should be assessed continually, and the next step set at just beyond the child's current capabilities. Initially, time spent in the water should be brief, especially if the child is showing signs of feeling cold or tired.

Always leave the pool with a child who wanted to stay a little longer (even if this makes for a slightly fractious departure!).

Gaining in confidence in the water is an important part of learning to swim.

DEVELOPING INDEPENDENCE

As progress is made, the need for buoyancy aids gets less. It gradually becomes possible to reduce the amount of air in the aids, and eventually to remove them completely so that the child is beginning to swim completely unaided. Before children can be allowed to move freely around the shallow end of the pool, they must be able to regain a standing position from both the front and back swimming positions. This is an important safety measure.

STANDING POSITION FROM THE FRONT

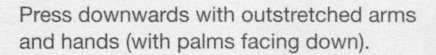

Floating on the front.

Press downwards with outstretched arms and hands (with palms facing down).

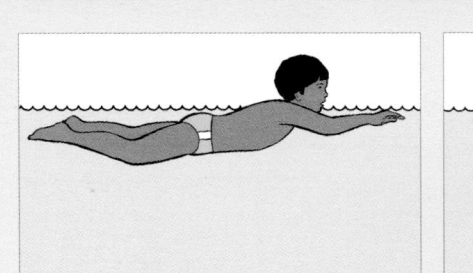

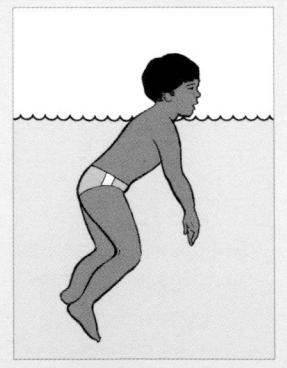

Tilt the head back and bend the knees forwards.

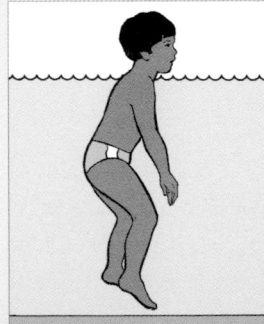

As the body becomes upright, push the feet downwards to stand, while using the arms to help maintain balance.

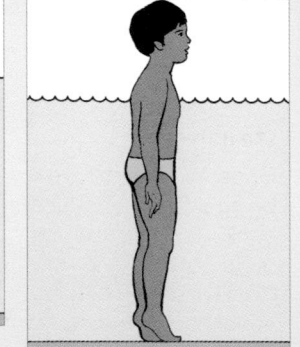

Stand on the bottom.

STANDING POSITION FROM THE BACK

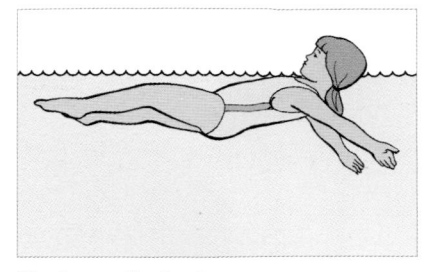

Floating on the back.

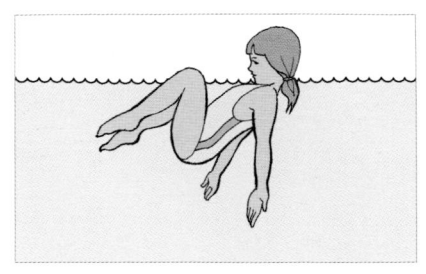

Lift the head forwards, pressing down with the arms.

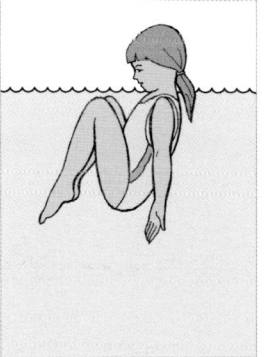

At the same time, raise the knees towards the chest.

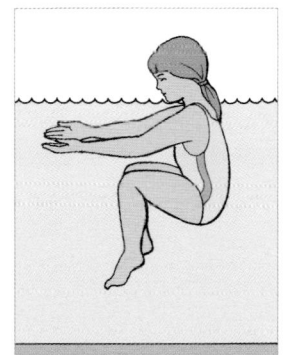

As the body rotates to an upright position, turn palms to face the feet and scoop the arms forwards and upwards to assist the movement.

Push the feet downwards to stand.

The next step

Once beginners have a 100 per cent record at being able to stand from both the front and the back floating positions, they are ready to move on to pushing and gliding.

This enables beginner swimmers to experience movement through the water in a stretched and streamlined position, which is fundamental to all swimming strokes.

Although the illustrations show children, these first steps are useful for anyone learning to swim.

GLIDING

Being able to glide through the water is a key swimming skill. Even the best swimmers – Olympic or world champions – keep a sense of gliding in their stroke. Being able to slide through the water efficiently, rather than ploughing through it, gives them greater speed.

The front glide

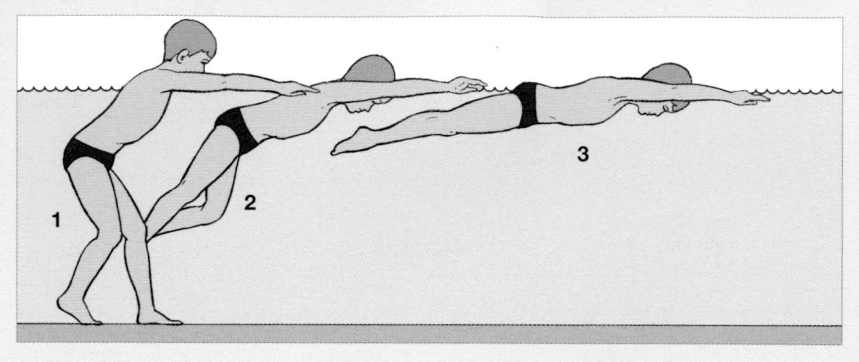

1 Start from a standing position, with one foot slightly in front of the other, arms extended forwards and shoulders submerged.

2 Lean forwards, push along the surface and glide.

3 Keep your head in line with your body, so that the top of your head is always at water level.

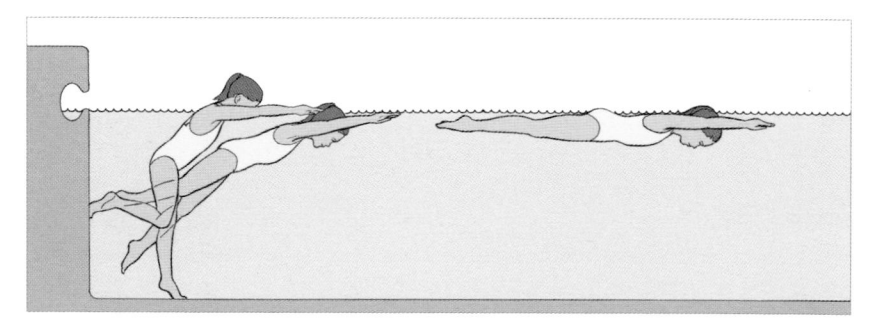

To increase the distance, start with your back against the poolside. Plant one foot firmly on the wall of the pool to obtain a stronger push.

Practising

Once they have been learned separately, it's a good idea to practise gliding and standing at the same time. This gets learner swimmers used to standing up while moving through the water, which is useful when they start learning to swim on the front or back.

The back glide

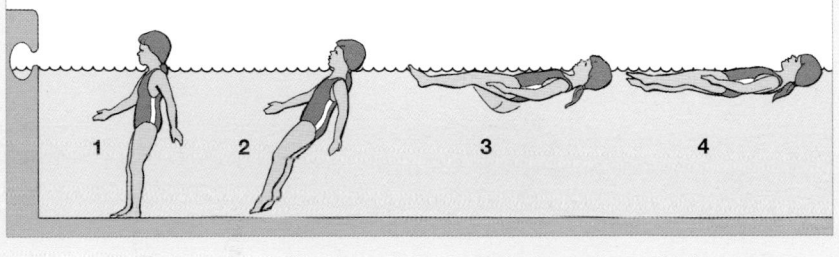

1 From a standing position, with one foot slightly to the rear of the other, lower your body until your shoulders are submerged. Keep your arms spread out to help with balance.

2 Lean gently backwards and at the same time push into a glide.

3 The back of your head should rest in the water.

4 Bring your arms to your sides.

> For more streamlining and greater distance, push with your arms stretched beyond your head and hands together.

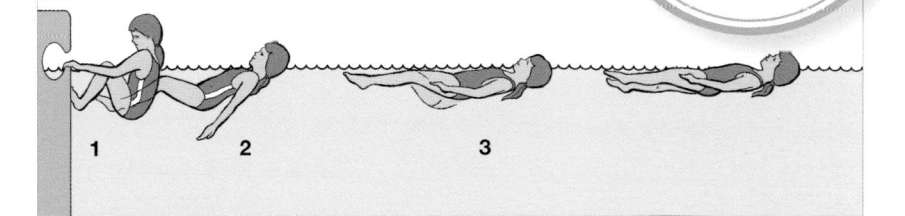

1 For greater distance, start by holding on to the poolside, with your feet placed firmly against the wall of the pool and knees just below the surface.

2 Release your hands from the poolside and push with your legs.

3 Tuck in your arms and bring your legs up to a gliding position, in which your body should remain flat.

THE PADDLE STROKES

Once learner swimmers have become confident with gliding and standing up, the time has come to learn basic actions for swimming on the front and the back. These usually take the form of the front paddle (which used to be called the doggie paddle) and the back paddle.

Front paddle

The leg action is similar to the alternating up and down movement used for the front crawl.

The arm action takes place totally underwater. One arm, then the other, is pulled downwards and backwards from the forward position.

Each arm returns to the front by stretching the hands forwards, from close to the chest to a point ahead of the shoulders.

Initially, the swimmer will probably make short arm movements, but as confidence grows these actions will become longer and more powerful.

Feel for the water

Developing a 'feel' for the water is an important part of becoming a successful swimmer. When swimmers talk about 'feel', they mean the way they catch hold of the water with their hands and lever themselves forward.

Back paddle

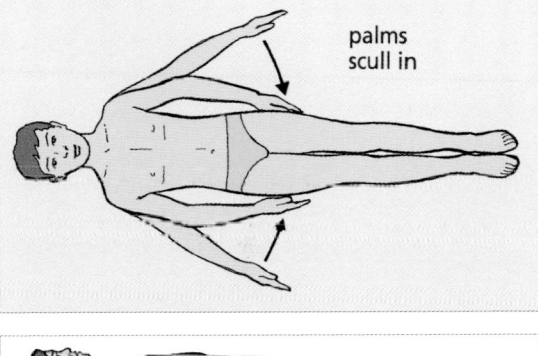

palms
scull in

The leg action is similar to the alternating up and down movement used for backstroke.

Most people start with arm movements of simultaneous sweeping actions towards the feet. Whilst this action produces considerable power, the recovery also creates a great deal of resistance.

Gradually, learners start to keep the arms closer to the thighs: their movements become more like a figure-of-eight sculling action.

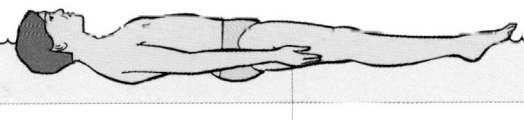

On the inward sweep, the thumbs are raised, so that the palms face inwards and downwards.

palms
scull out

At the outer and innermost points in the action the wrists rotate, to change the angle of the palms.

As the hands move away from the body, the little fingers are raised so that the palms are facing outwards and downwards.

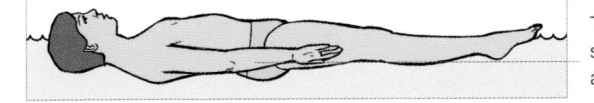

The arms remain fairly straight and as relaxed as possible.

This is the oldest of the four major strokes and is frequently used in recreational swimming, lifesaving and competition.

SEQUENCE

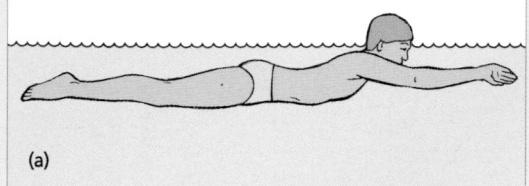 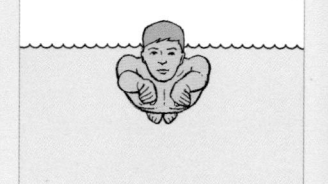

(a)

Before starting the stroke, the swimmer is on their front in a streamlined and horizontal position, with their shoulders parallel to the surface of the water. The head is in line with the body, and looking ahead, along or just below the surface of the water. The arms are extended in front and close together underwater; the legs are trailed out behind, straight and together.

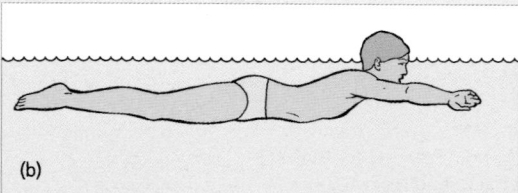 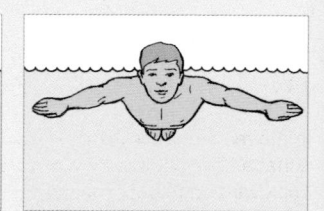

(b)

The stroke begins with the arms pulling outwards, backwards and downwards to a point just in front of the shoulders. The legs remain stretched out behind.

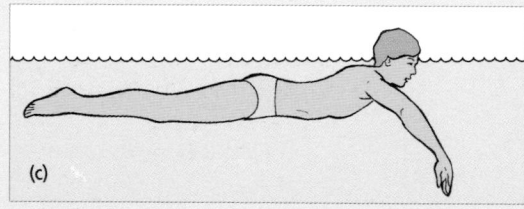 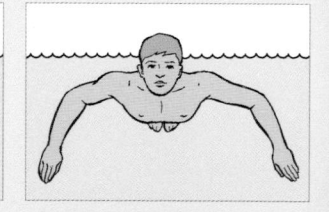

(c)

In front of the shoulder-line the hands begin to sweep inwards with a swirling action, coming close together with the elbows close to the body ready to start the recovery action.

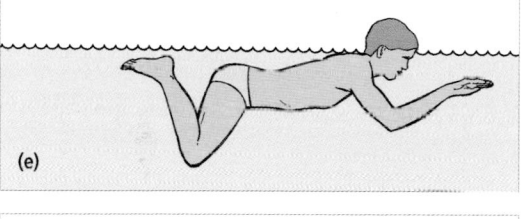 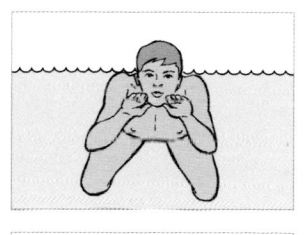

(d)

As the arms sweep in, the legs are brought up and feet turned out, ready for the next leg kick. At this point the swimmer usually breathes in, as the mouth is clear of the water.

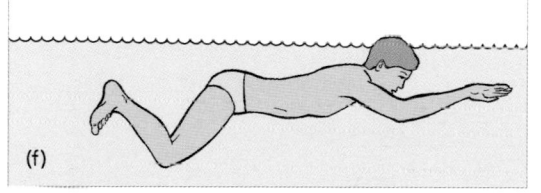 

(e)

(f)

In the recovery, the arms are extended forwards, usually on or just under the surface. At the same time the feet begin their new kick, thrusting vigorously backwards and outwards in an accelerating movement. They whip together and end with the toes pointed backwards. This drives the swimmer forward and allows them to glide ahead with their arms outstretched, ready for the next stroke.

Timing your leg and arm movements correctly is the key to swimming breaststroke well. If you can feel your leg recovery creating drag, your timing is out!

PRACTICES

Body position

- Holding the rail or trough, practise the leg action briefly.

- With a float held out in front, swim across the width of the pool using legs only.

- Push and glide, followed by leg action only.

Arm action

- Leaning forward in shallow water with shoulders submerged, practise the arm action.

- Grip a float between your thighs and try swimming arms-only.

Breathing and timing

- Push and glide, lifting your head to breathe as you make your inwards arm stroke.

- Once you are comfortable with one breath, add a leg kick and glide before standing up.

- Next, add a second arm stroke and breath.

- Add more strokes until you establish a comfortable rhythm.

HANDY HINTS

Body position

- Aim for a stretched, streamlined and near-horizontal position. Keep your head steady and shoulders square; hips just below the surface; legs extended; toes pointed.

Leg action

- Your heels lead the backward drive. The feet must be turned outwards for the final drive; the leg kick must be simultaneous and symmetrical.

- The leg recovery takes place under water, with toes pointed back.

- Keep your legs behind the line of your hips at all times.

Arm action

- Keep your hands in view all the time.

- Pull in front of the shoulders, pressing strongly sideways, downwards and then in, recovering smoothly.

Breathing

- Inhale as the arms complete their pull; exhale as you glide forwards.

Timing

- Aim for a strong kick backwards and a smooth glide to follow.

- As the arms are extended forwards, the legs drive backwards vigorously.

COMPETITION RULES

There are a number of points to remember when swimming the breaststroke competitively.

- From the beginning of the first arm stroke after the start and after each turn, the body must be kept horizontal and the shoulders parallel with the water surface.

- All hand and feet movements must be simultaneous and in the same horizontal plane, without any alternating movements.

- Part of the head must be above the water level during each complete stroke cycle (except when starting and turning).

- Up-and-down movements of the legs are not allowed.

The combination of drive and glide is the key to swimming breaststroke well.

FRONT CRAWL

Front crawl is the fastest of all the swimming strokes, partly because both arms and legs provide continuous power. Throughout the stroke the swimmer keeps a horizontal and streamlined body position, with the head in line with the body, eyes looking forwards and downwards and legs and feet extended.

SEQUENCE

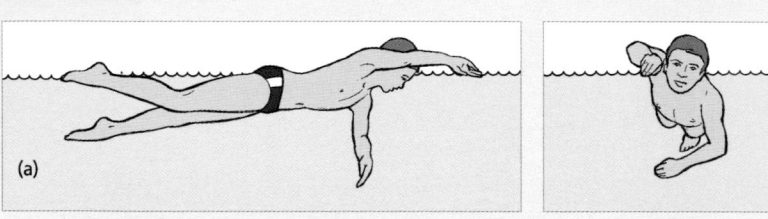

(a)

The right hand enters the water in front of the head and mid-way between the shoulder and the head. The arm action is alternating and continuous. The hand gradually accelerates downwards and along (and finally upwards) through the water. The arm recovers over the water with a high elbow movement, extending forwards slightly in preparation for re-entry.

Front crawl leg kick is alternating and vertical, with legs passing close together. The movement starts in the hips and finishes with a whip-like action of the feet.

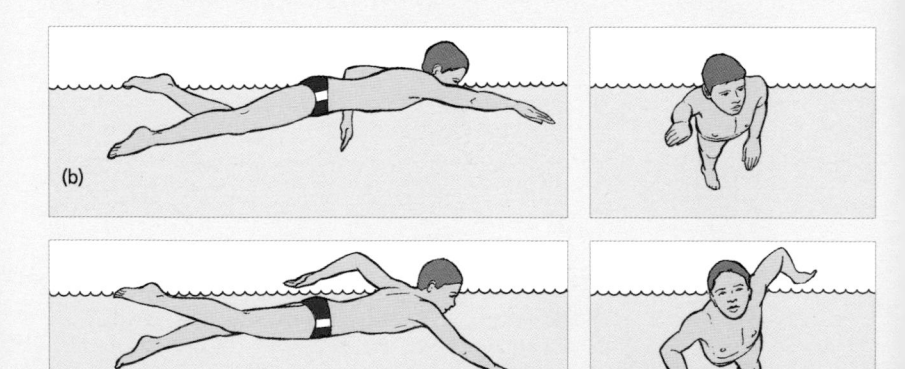

(b)

(c)

As the right arm sweeps downwards, the left sweeps upwards through the water into the recovery (see diagrams b and c). The strong downsweep of the right arm is balanced by a kick of the left leg (see diagram c).

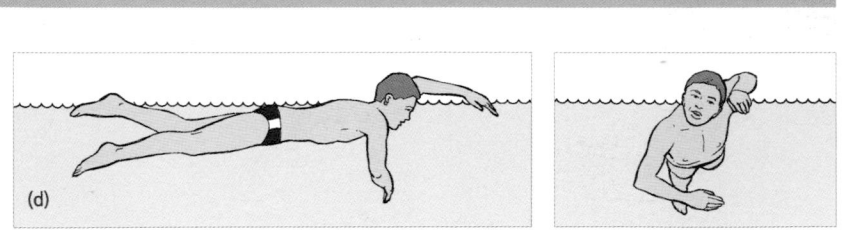

(d)

After the downsweep, the right arm sweeps inwards while the left completes the recovery.

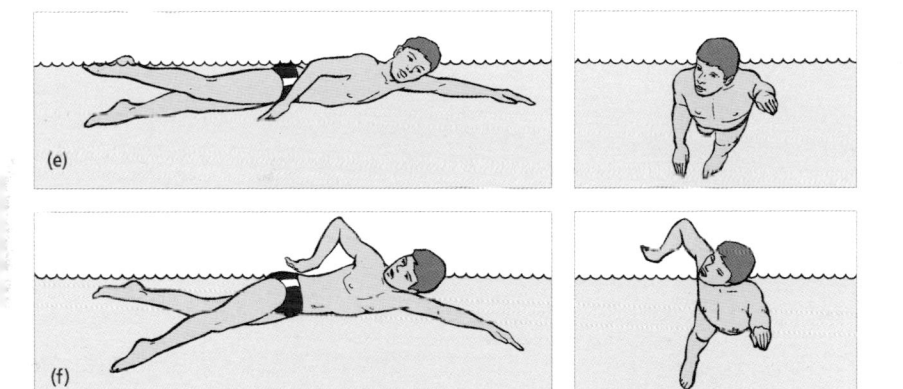

(e)

(f)

As the left hand extends forwards to start the downsweep, the right arm sweeps upwards towards the recovery. The head turns to the right, synchronised with the natural roll of the body. This enables the swimmer to inhale as the right arm recovers. (While moving through the water at speed, the head creates a bow wave and a trough behind it, which lets the swimmer inhale clear of the water without lifting their head.)

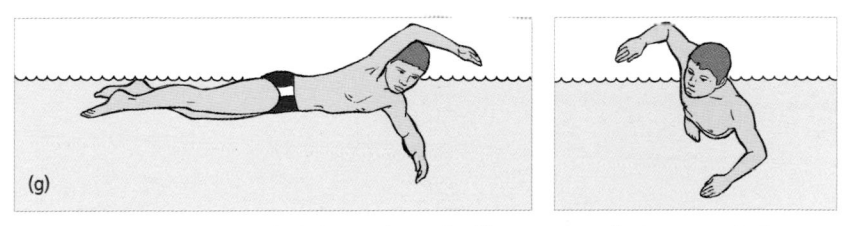

(g)

After breathing in, the eyes look forwards again. The sequence is then repeated. Some swimmers find it natural to breathe with the head turned to the left; others learn to breathe on both sides. These are both equally good techniques.

PRACTICES

Leg action

- Practise the leg action briefly at the poolside, holding the rail or trough with your face below the surface.

- Holding a float out in front of you, swim along legs-only.

Arm action

- Leaning forwards in shallow water with shoulders submerged, copy a demonstration of the arm action.

- Push and glide, add the leg action, and then introduce one complete arm cycle.

- Repeat, increasing the number of full stroke-cycles.

Breathing

- Practise standing in shallow water, leaning forwards and grasping the rail or trough with one hand, with your face in the water. Breathe out into the water, then turn your head away from the supporting arm to breathe in quickly. Return your head to the forward position and repeat the practice.

- Hold a float. Push off and add a leg kick. Use one arm to pull. Turn the head to breathe as the arm finishes its pull. Change hands.

- Swim a full stroke, attempting one or two breaths during each width.

Timing

- Normally there are six leg kicks to each complete arm-cycle, but variations of this are OK as long as the leg action balances that of the arm action (for example, four kicks to each arm-cycle).

The arms and legs deliver power throughout the stroke.

HANDY HINTS

Body position

- Aim for a stretched, streamlined and horizontal position.

Leg action

- Keep your legs straight and close together, ankles loose; feel the kick passing through your knee and ending in a whip-like action of your foot.

Arm action

- Your hand enters the water thumb and fingers first, elbow high.
- Aim for a smooth, flowing action, with relaxed arm recovery over the water.

Breathing

- Water should be level with your forehead. Eyes open, looking forwards.
- Breathe out through your nose and mouth into the water.
- Rotate your head so that your mouth is just clear of the water when breathing in.

Timing

- At first it's best to practise over short distances several times. As your style becomes more efficient, you will find that you can swim further.

▼ One of the world's best-ever swimmers, Ian Thorpe of Australia, demonstrating a nice, relaxed front crawl recovery action.

BACKSTROKE

Backstroke is like front crawl in that the arm and leg movements both alternate, allowing continuous forward power. Although this stroke is not as fast as the front crawl, when performed well it can be graceful and fluent. The arms recover over the water, and the legs kick up and down. Throughout the stroke the body maintains a near-horizontal position, with the back of the head pillowed in the water and the hips just below the surface.

SEQUENCE

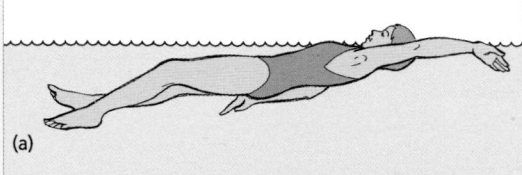

(a)

The swimmer maintains a flat and streamlined body position, with the head in line with the body. The left arm enters the water ready to sweep downwards and outwards. At this point, the right arm has finished the second downward sweep and is about to leave the water for recovery.

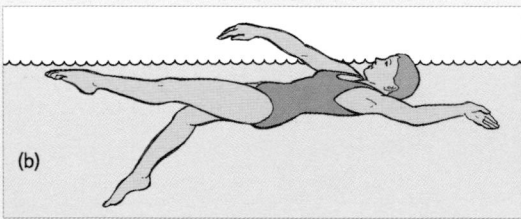

(b)

As the left arm sweeps downwards and outwards it bends gradually at the elbow. The right arm is lifted upwards and straight ahead.

As in front crawl, your feet keep up a constant kicking rhythm, usually six or four beats per stroke cycle.

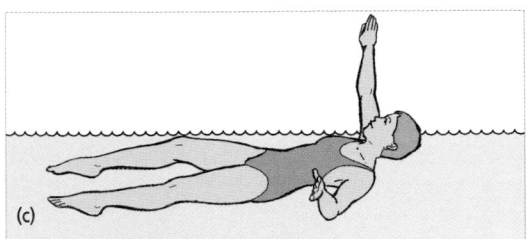

(c) Underwater, the left arm continues to bend as it sweeps upwards, reaching an angle of approximately 90°. The right arm is now overhead.

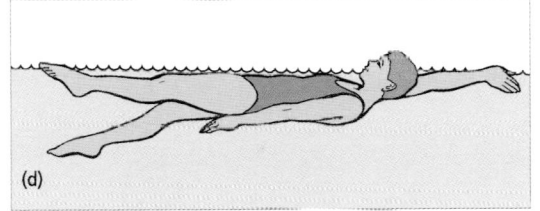

(d) The left arm now finishes its propulsive phase, just as the fully extended right arm enters the water directly in advance of the shoulder.

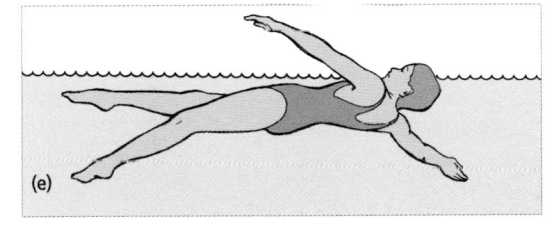

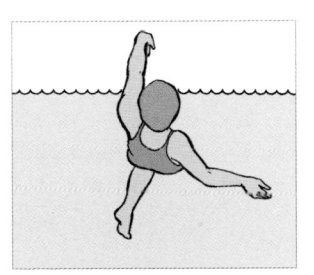

(e) The right arm is now starting its propulsive phase, and the left arm begins its recovery.

Top backstroke swimmers aim to keep their head perfectly still and in line with their body at all times.

PRACTICES

These practices or 'drills' will help you begin to develop a fast, smooth backstroke. Having a smooth stroke is one of the keys to swimming fast backstroke.

Body position

- Push off and glide on your back with your arms extended beyond your head.

Leg action

- With a float under each arm, push off and add the leg action.

- With a float held at arm's length above your head, glide into position and add the leg action.

Arm action

- Push and glide from the poolside, add the leg action to establish body position, then introduce the arms.

- Attempt a few strokes at a time. Increase the distance swum gradually.

Breathing

- While swimming full-stroke, breathe regularly; breathe in as one arm recovers and breathe out as the other recovers.

HANDY HINTS

Body position

- Keep the back of your head in the water and don't look down at your feet! Keep your hips at the surface.

- Keep your body flat, with arms and legs extended.

Leg action

- Move the legs from the hips.

- Keep the knees below the surface.

- The ankles should feel flexed and loose, and the toes should just break the surface.

Arm action

- Maintain a continuous, alternating arm action with one arm in an approximately opposite position to the other.

Timing

- Aim for continuous action without any pauses: a relaxed arm recovery will help you achieve this.

Good backstroke position: body flat and head still and pillowed in the water.

BUTTERFLY STROKE

The butterfly is the second-fastest stroke and also the 'youngest'. It is usually the last to be learned because it requires a high degree of strength, mobility and coordination.

The swimmer is in a prone position, and both arms and legs are in continuous movement. The arms recover over the water, and the legs kick up and down together. The body moves in an undulating or dolphin-like pattern, with the head rising above the water to breathe at the end of the underwater arm-pull. The hands trace a series of sculling actions in the water: they sweep out, down, in, and finally out again to exit the water by the thighs.

SEQUENCE

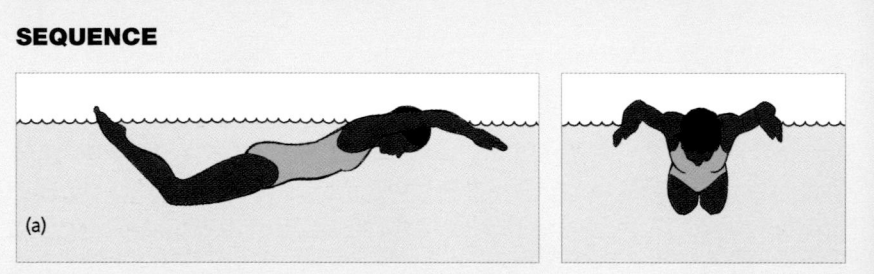

(a)

The hands enter the water with the thumbs and fingers first, about shoulder-width apart. The legs are beginning the first down beat.

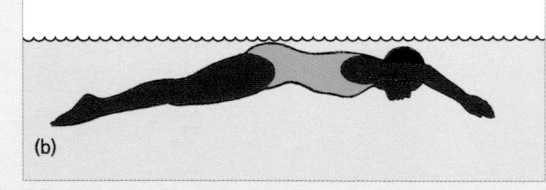

(b)

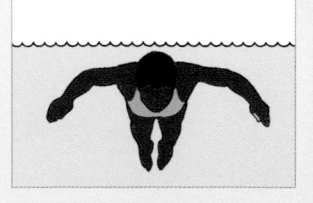

At the end of the outsweep, the arms start the downsweep with elbows uppermost as the legs complete the first down beat.

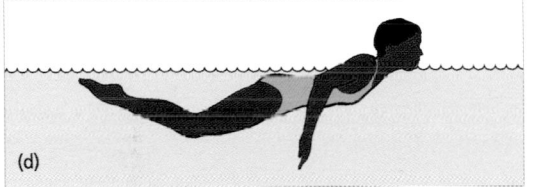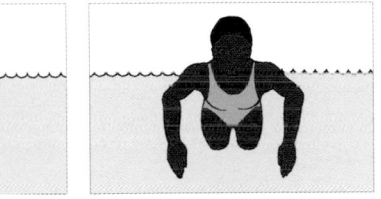

(c)

The arms have completed the down and insweep and the legs have risen to the surface in readiness for the next propulsive down kick.

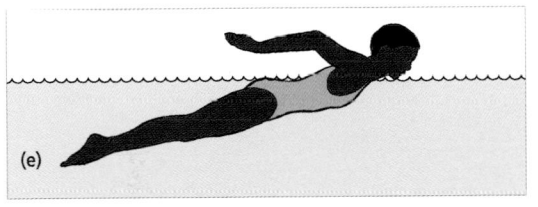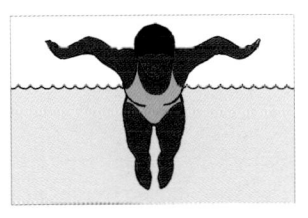

(d)

After the arms have passed the line of the shoulders, they sweep outwards and accelerate to their fastest underwater speed. The legs are beginning the second down beat.

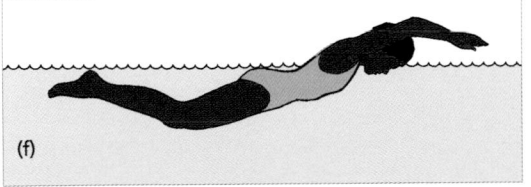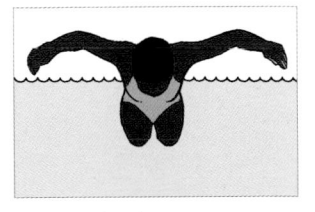

(e)

As an extension of the final outsweep of the hands and arms, the elbows lead the recovery. The legs finish their second downward thrust. The upper body is at its highest position, making it easier for the swimmer to inhale at this stage.

(f)

The arms recover low with the elbows slightly bent in preparation for the entry. The legs return to the surface while the head moves back into the water.

PRACTICES

Body position

- Push off and glide with your arms outstretched, on your front, back and side, undulating like a fish.

Leg action

- Holding a float with your arms extended in front, briefly practise a front-crawl-type leg action with the feet and ankles kicking together, instead of one at a time.

- Repeat, but using a short breaststroke arm action instead of a float.

Arm action

- Standing firmly with the body bent forwards and the shoulders in the water, practise the arm action.

Breathing

- Practise the arm action with your face in the water. Then raise your chin up and forwards, to breathe in as your arms push your body out of the water.

Timing

- Push off and glide. Perform two leg kicks, followed by two more with an arm pull and recovery.

- Repeat, increasing the number of cycles. Gradually introduce breathing into every cycle.

HANDY HINTS

Body position

- Start by using this stroke over short distances. Initiate the kicking movement from the hips.

Leg action

- Your leg action should help to keep a good, flat body position. Kick from the hips, drive the feet down vigorously and maintain a continuous action.

- Try to keep relaxed ankles.

Arm action

- Feel your arms sweeping back over the water to recover with elbows uppermost in a 'flinging' action. Your hands should enter the water about shoulder-width apart.

Breathing

- Hold your breath and then exhale explosively immediately before breathing in. Do this at the end of the upsweep, when your mouth is clear of the water.

Timing

- Make the first kick as the arms begin the outsweep, and the second as the arms are completing the upsweep.

COMPETITION RULES

In competition, all movements of the arms must be simultaneous. The arms must be taken forwards over the surface and brought back under the surface. The body must be kept horizontal with the shoulder aligned from the beginning of the first arm action after the start and turns. All movements of the feet must be simultaneous, not alternating.

> **Top butterfly swimmers try to keep their body as flat in the water as possible, even when breathing.**

Steve Parry of Great Britain just about to begin his arm recovery. Even though his head is up and forward, his body is still reasonably flat in the water.

DIVING

Diving is a very popular (and fun!) activity among young swimmers and offers fast pool entry for those moving towards competitive training.

Including diving skills in your learn-to-swim lesson adds variety, but it is important to understand the safety aspects. At its very worst, diving can result in spinal injuries and even paralysis. But if you follow the safety guidelines, you can be confident of diving free from major injury.

The majority of accidents happen as a result of diving into shallow water or colliding with other swimmers. In open water, accidents usually occur when people dive into water of unknown depth (usually because of murky conditions) or collide with submerged obstacles. This chapter outlines the key safety aspects of diving and includes practices for learning to dive, up to and including the plunge dive.

SAFETY CHECKS

Before diving, take great care to ensure that the water is deep enough and that the diving area is clear of swimmers. 'No Diving' notices will be prominently displayed in all pools or areas of pools where there is a vertical depth of less than 1.5m. Key safety points to remember are:

- check that the minimum water depth for headfirst entries is 1.8m

- check the distance between the poolside and the surface of the water (maximum 0.38m)

- check the distance from the starting point to the opposite wall (you need at least 7.6m).

- Check that the diving area is clearly marked across the pool (for example with rope dividers).

> **Diving should only be conducted in the presence of a qualified, knowledgeable and experienced teacher in a swimming pool of suitable water depth.**

DIVING CODE

Before learning how to dive, it is important to know and understand the diving code. The code requires that divers:

- check the entry area is clear before starting to dive

- always dive and glide with arms extended

- swim away from the starting position and avoid crossing the path of another diver after resurfacing

- work in pairs and observe partners carefully

- avoid pushing

- do not wear goggles.

Britain's Kerri-Anne Payne dives into the pool in competition.

LEARNING HOW TO DIVE

Many people are not confident immediately submerging, gliding underwater and returning to the surface. If this is the case, try the five activities that are listed here while standing in shallow water. They are designed to get learners used to being underwater, and eventually upside-down, before attempting a headfirst entry from the poolside.

- Hold on to the trough or poolside, placing the face in the water and blowing bubbles.

- Pick up objects from the bottom of the pool (for example coloured rings, balls).

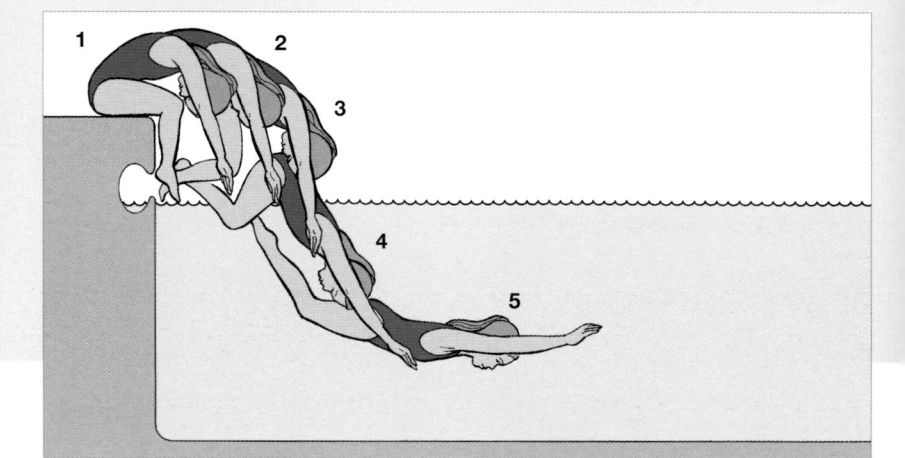

Never learn to dive unless you are confident swimming in water of 1.8m depth or more, as this is the minimum safe depth for diving.

Sitting dive

1 Take a sitting position on the poolside, with your feet together resting on the trough.

2 Next, bend your body forwards with your head held down between outstretched arms.

3 By raising your hips and leaning further forwards, overbalance into a shallow dive.

4 Next, plunge headfirst into the water.

5 Arch your back to go forwards.

- Push and glide to the bottom of the pool, then return to the surface by raising your head and pointing your hands upwards.

- Try a handstand in waist-deep water.

- Spring over or through apparatus (hoop or float) from a standing position in the water with the arms extended above the head. Spring into a handstand or take a shallower, oblique entry into a glide.

When the learners can perform the above activities confidently, they are ready to progress to headfirst entries from the poolside.

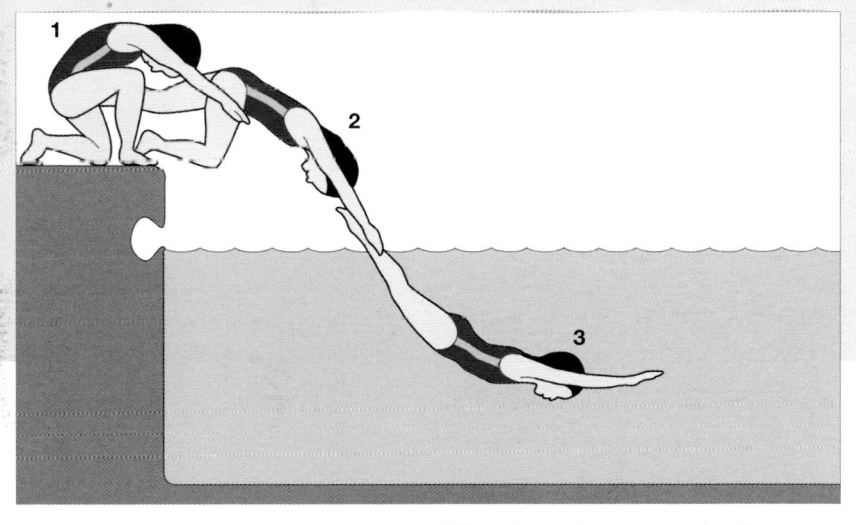

Kneeling dive

1 Place one foot forwards, toes gripping the edge of the pool, with the other knee alongside your foot.

2 Holding your head firmly between your upper arms, bend towards the water (still keeping the arms extended and the head down). Raise your hips and allow your body to overbalance. Try to aim for the bottom of the pool.

3 Stretch your legs on entering the water and glide back to the surface with your arms extended.

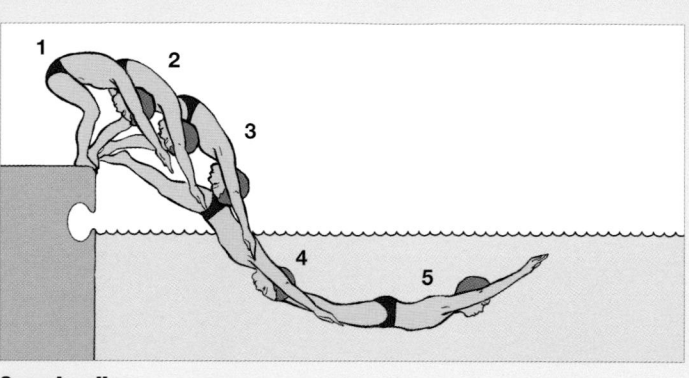

Crouch roll

The crouch roll is the first standing dive many people learn.

1 Crouch on the poolside, knees and feet together and toes gripping the edge. Press your arms tightly to your ears and point down towards the water, with your chin on your chest.

2, 3, 4, 5 Roll your body forwards smoothly and reach for the bottom of the pool.

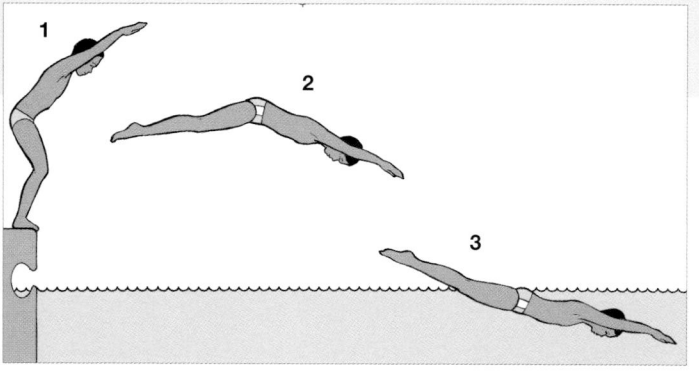

Crouch dive

1 Take a more upright position, knees bent together and toes gripping the edge of the pool. Press your upper arms firmly against your head, hands pointed out towards the water.

2 Lean forwards so that you overbalance; then give a strong upward push through the hips with your feet.

3 Aim to enter the water further away from the poolside than for the crouch roll. The resulting glide should be shallower.

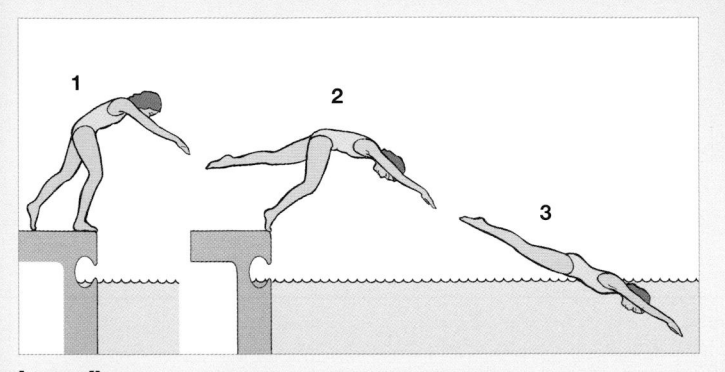

Lunge dive

1 Place one foot at the edge of the pool, toes gripping the edge. The other foot is stretched behind, toes just touching the floor.

2 Bend towards the water, keeping your head and arms in line. Slowly raise your back leg until your body overbalances.

3 As your hands reach the water, your front leg joins the other to give a good entry position. The aim should be to glide for even further.

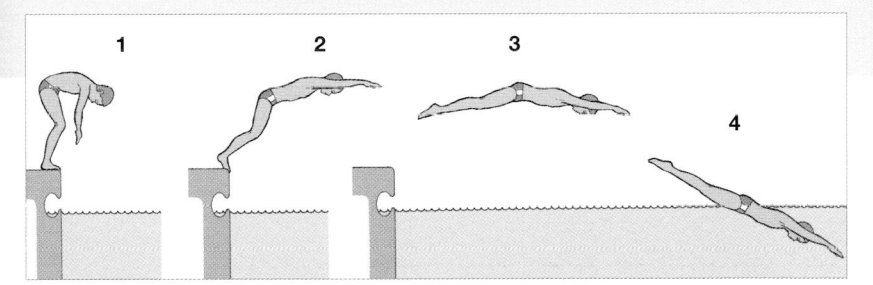

Plunge dive

1 Stand with your feet slightly apart and toes gripping the edge, with your body bent downwards. Let your arms hang loosely down.

2 When you start to overbalance, swing your arms forwards. At the same time, push strongly forwards with your legs.

3 During flight, your body should be fully extended and almost straight, in order to achieve a clean entry

4 This dive is often used for poolside entries, so it is worth practising it until you are confident.

> **Look at the place where you want to enter the water.**

NON-COMPETITION STROKES

In addition to front crawl, backstroke, breaststroke and butterfly, there are other strokes that are no longer used in competition. They are worth learning for fun, as well as because some are useful in activities such as lifesaving.

ELEMENTARY BACKSTROKE

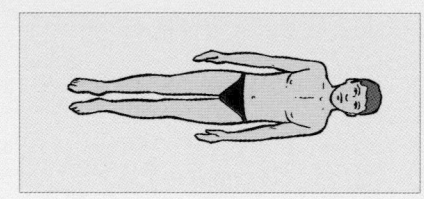

(a)

Body position

Lying on your back, take up an almost horizontal position. Your face should be clear of the water and your legs slightly submerged (so that your knees won't break the surface on recovery).

The leg action is like an upside-down breaststroke, with flexed ankles and the kick is felt in the soles of the feet.

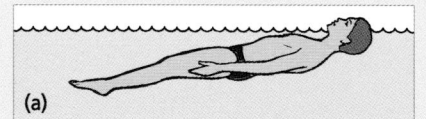

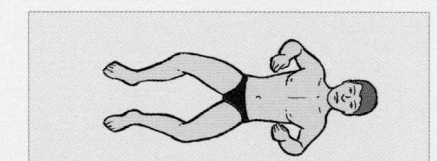

(b)

Recovery

Bend your knees by dropping your lower legs (heels moving towards your bottom). Your heels should be hip-width or more apart, ready for the drive backwards. On completion of the recovery, your feet should be flexed and turned out, ready for propulsion.

The arm action is like a wide sculling action. Keep your hands underwater and move them simultaneously. Pull them upwards, close to your body, from thigh to chest. Then sweep them sideways until the arms are extended in line with the shoulders, ready for the arm pull.

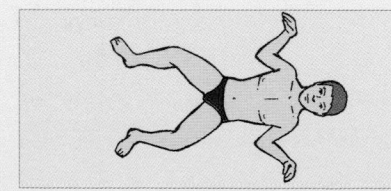

(c)

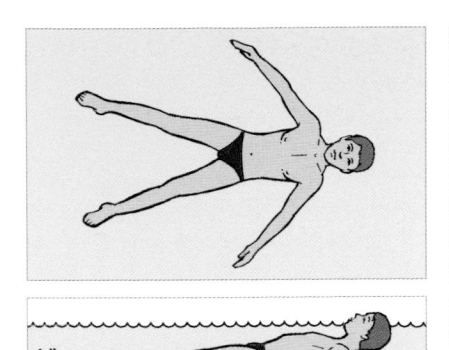

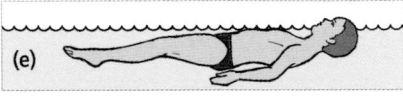

(d)

(e)

Propulsion

With your heels well apart and the ankles flexed, drive slightly out and back. Your feet follow a circular path, with the inside edges as well as the sides of the feet pushing against the water. Next, bring your legs together in a streamlined position for the glide.

For the arm pull, use the palms of your hands to 'catch' the water. With extended arms, press strongly backwards and inwards towards the sides of your body.

TIMING

Leg movements tend to come before arm actions (though they appear to be happening together). There is no pause between the end of recovery and the beginning of propulsion. A glide may be performed with the body held in an extended position at the end of the propulsive actions.

Breathe on recovery and exhale with propulsion, keeping your face clear of the water throughout the stroke.

SIDESTROKE

Sidestroke is a useful stroke for anyone who is interested in learning lifesaving skills. A combination of this and lifesaving backstroke can be used for towing people who have got into trouble in the water back to the safety of dry land.

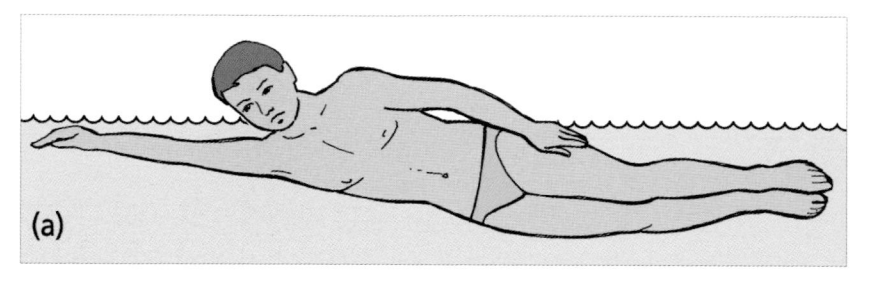

(a)

Body position

As the name suggests, for this stroke you lie in the water on your side, in as streamlined and horizontal a position as possible. The side of your head is in the water; your eyes and nose are just above the surface. During the glide, your upper arm lies along the upper side of your body and your lower arm is extended forwards, in advance of your head.

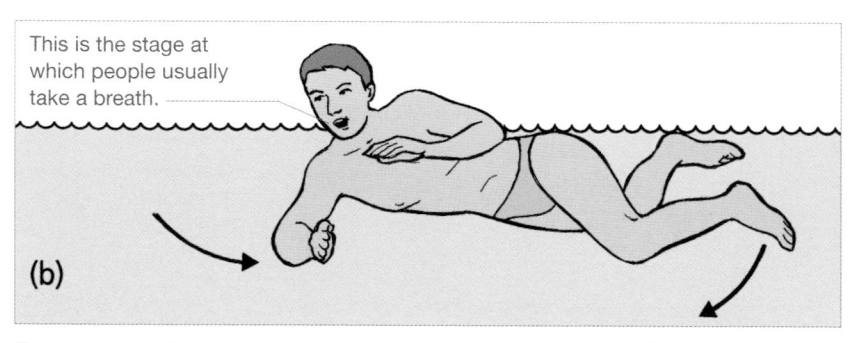

This is the stage at which people usually take a breath.

(b)

The legs move simultaneously, one above the other and extended. The upper leg moves forwards and the lower leg moves backwards, with the knees bending and the heels moving towards the seat.

   Your upper arm recovers as it moves forwards to a position with elbow bent and hand below your head. At the same time your lower arm propels, by pulling in a downward-sideways direction to meet the other arm, in a similar position, with elbow bent and the hand below the head.

Timing

While your arms are moving inwards to their bent positions, your legs recover from their extended bent positions ready for the propulsive kick. At the same time, you extend your arms. Then there is a short glide before the actions are repeated.

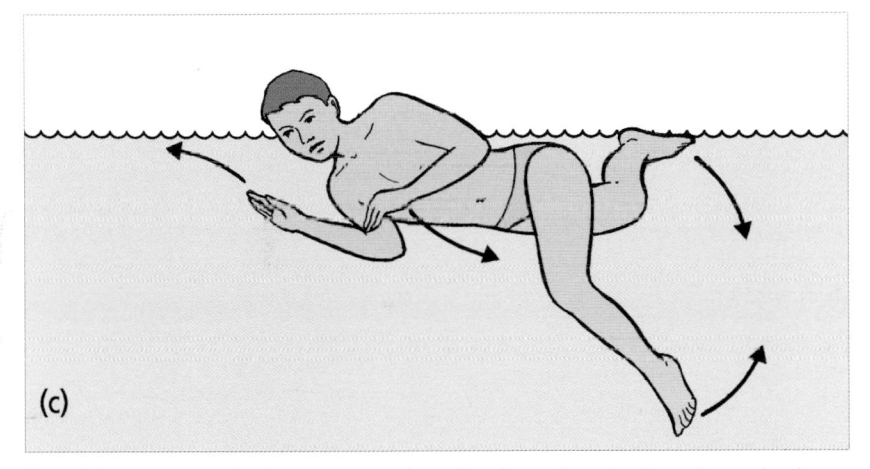

(c)

Propulsion occurs as the legs are swept together through a circular pathway, back to the extended position that is held during a glide. The action is sometimes called a 'scissor' kick.

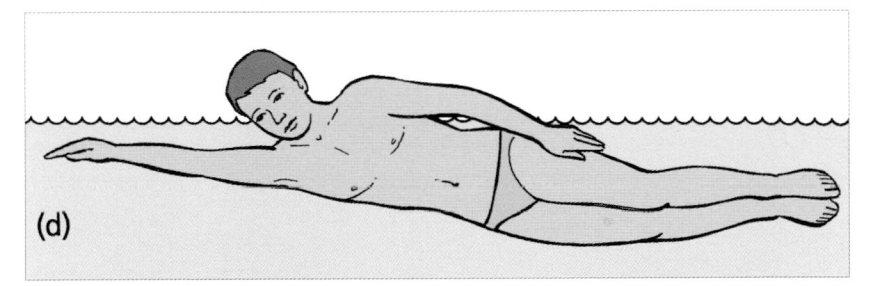

(d)

Your arms move simultaneously and without pausing. They should now be extended, with the upper arm propelling as it pushes downwards-backwards and the lower arm recovering as it extends to the forwards position.

SWIMMING WITH DISABILITIES

Because of the support that the water offers, swimming can allow people living with disabilities to experience success and enjoyment that may not be possible for them in other environments. Unless their condition precludes it, there is no reason why people with disabilities should not go swimming as often as anyone else.

FACILITIES

All swimming pools have special facilities for people with disabilities, including access to buildings, changing facilities and the pool itself. They can also usually recommend appropriately qualified teachers and assistants. These are important, because while the aims of teaching swimming are the same for everyone, teaching methods and activities need to be tailored to the specific needs of individuals.

FIRST VISITS

For many people, a first visit to the swimming pool can be a traumatic time. Anxiety can result in various ways – excitement, aggression, tears, and even withdrawal. There are a number of things to consider for anyone teaching or helping a person with a disability to learn to swim.

- Maintain a positive, confident approach, especially if the learner swimmer is initially nervous. This will help reduce fear and anxiety levels.

- Be seen to have a concern for safety, which again will help provide reassurance in the face of nervousness.

While specific disabilities require individual approaches, a number of activities are generally useful. These include bobbing and breathing; water adjustment and floating; perceptual motor activities; basic safety skills; swimming skills; and games activities with and without music.

SWIMMING CLUBS

There are many swimming clubs that can help people with disabilities develop their skills. These are also good places to meet similarly minded people. There is a growing and lively competition circuit for swimmers with disabilities. Anyone wanting to race will find a club a good source of help and information.

BASIC SKILLS

Learning the following skills builds self-confidence and water competence, as well as helping people learn swimming skills:

- safe water entry and exit (with the use of an appropriate lifting procedure if needed)

- flotation

- recovery to a safe resting position and place

- rhythmic breathing

- changing direction whilst in the water.

British swimmer Sarah Bailey in action at the Athens Paralympics.

WATER SAFETY

Water safety is the promotion of understanding how to be safe in and near water. It is an important part of the National Curriculum. Some aspects of water safety can be learned at home or in class. It can even be learned before the first visit to the pool by anyone old enough to understand the principles. Indeed, the principles of water safety can start around the home and garden.

Water safety can be interesting and challenging, especially if people use their imagination regarding potentially dangerous situations. The principles associated with water safety can be reinforced at any time you are near an expanse of water, or even when a favourite television programme involves some aquatic activity.

The following rules can be reinforced and understood using a few simple questions. The questions aim to get people thinking about the reasons behind the rules:

Rule	Reinforcing question
1) When playing in or near water, always have a strong older swimmer with you.	**1)** Why is it a good idea to swim with other people?
2) Learn the beach-flag code.	**2)** What colour flags mark safe swimming areas? What colour flags suggest dangerous water?
3) If you are in trouble in water, relax, roll on to your back, and if you see somebody wave with one arm to attract attention. Otherwise, keep your arms under the water.	**3)** If someone in the water is waving with one hand, what could it mean?
4) Don't go swimming in the hour after a heavy meal.	**4)** Why is it unwise to swim straight after a meal?

Lifeguards are there for your safety and you should always follow their advice to keep yourself safe.

SWIMMING ENVIRONMENTS

- Do not stand on the edge of a soft bank of a river, lake or stream: these can collapse, plunging you in.

- Do not play near or enter open water unless there is a lifeguard on duty.

- Never dive into unknown water: serious injuries can result, especially if you hit your head or neck.

- Don't use air beds in open water, they can be blown away from land.

- Learn the safety rules for swimming pools. In particular, never run, push people, or dive into a shallow area.

COLDNESS AND TIREDNESS

- If you feel cold or tired in the water, get out immediately. Coldness can quickly become hypothermia, which can cause death.

SAFETY CODE

Remember the Royal Life Saving Society's safety code:

- spot the dangers
- take safety advice
- go with a friend
- learn how to help.

SURVIVING DANGER

Over half the people who drown every year are within about 25m of the safety of land.

- Awareness of the basic principles of survival, combined with being able to swim 50m with confidence, could reduce the number of deaths.

- Most drownings happen as a result of 'fooling about' near water.

- Boys are far more likely to be involved in drowning accidents than girls.

All of this explains why swimming and water safety are vitally important, and why the school curriculum includes swimming, water safety and survival.

Research shows that even strong swimmers are only able to swim in cold water for short periods of time. This means they can cover only short distances; the colder the water, the shorter the distance. Depending on a victim's reaction to cold shock (see below), the maximum distance for swimming in water with a temperature around 4 or 5°C is 150m.

COLD SHOCK

'Cold shock' is the name given to the effects of sudden immersion in cold water on the body's systems. They are like an extreme version of standing under a very cold shower. The effects of cold shock are:

- a very rapid increase in the breathing rate (called 'hyperventilation'), which can be as much as five or six times faster than normal

- at the same time, blood pressure increases, accompanied by a narrowing of the blood vessels near the surface of the skin (called 'vasoconstriction'), which causes further increase in blood pressure.

The combination of these effects is to increase the output of blood from the heart by as much as 30 per cent. For many people, especially those who are less fit physically, this can be fatal.

SURVIVING THE COLD

How long anyone can survive in cold
water depends upon several factors:

- the physical and physiological
  characteristics of the individual

- the temperature and speed
  of flow of the water

- the distance from safety

- the expertise of any help available

- the swimming ability of
  the individual.

The aftermath of a
successful rescue.

ACTION IN AN EMERGENCY

Sudden immersion in cold water requires the 'casualty' to react quickly and confidently. The only way you can do this if you become a casualty is if you have already practised how to act in a safe environment. Practise the following.

1 Your first action should be to reduce the effect of cold shock by getting your breathing rate to return to near normal as quickly as possible. You can do this by taking deep, slow, controlled breaths, ideally while holding a floating object. If there is no floating object available, you may need to tread water. Use the least possible energy: a slow, steady movement similar to the breaststroke leg action is probably best (see the diagram on page 48).

2 If there has been some sort of accident, you then have to decide whether there is any danger from other sources such as oil, petrol or falling debris. If there is, swim away calmly and confidently, again using a breaststroke action to conserve energy.

3 Having reached relative safety it should be possible to look about and check for help close at hand. If there is, try to attract attention by using the International Distress Signal.

Where an emergency arises a few metres from the bank of a river or lake, a calm, confident swimmer should be able to take action to reduce the effects of cold shock and then wade or swim to the bank. However, it must be emphasised that, even in comparatively shallow water that is very cold, the effects of cold shock may be fatal for young children or older people.

The International
Distress Signal..

International Distress Signal:
while treading water, repeatedly raise one arm from an outstretched sideways position to a vertical position and back.

COMMONSENSE RULES FOR OPEN WATER

- Always use an approved life jacket when taking part in water sports.
- If a boat overturns, stay with it until help arrives.
- In an emergency away from the bank, retain as much clothing as possible. Remove only waterlogged garments that could cause you to sink.
- Keep your head above water as much as possible, and where possible use a floating object for support.

These students at a surf lifesaving class are learning to be beach lifeguards.

BASIC SURVIVAL

Treading water

Being able to tread water means you can stay in a vertically upright position with your head above water. The most effective technique in a survival situation is a slow, steady breaststroke leg action while sculling with outstretched arms.

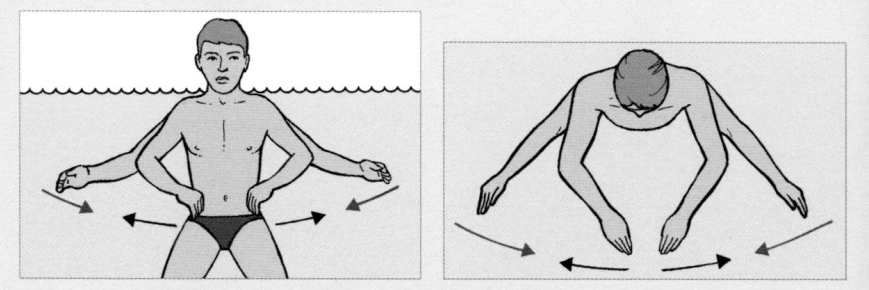

The arm movement is a gentle sculling action, in and out.

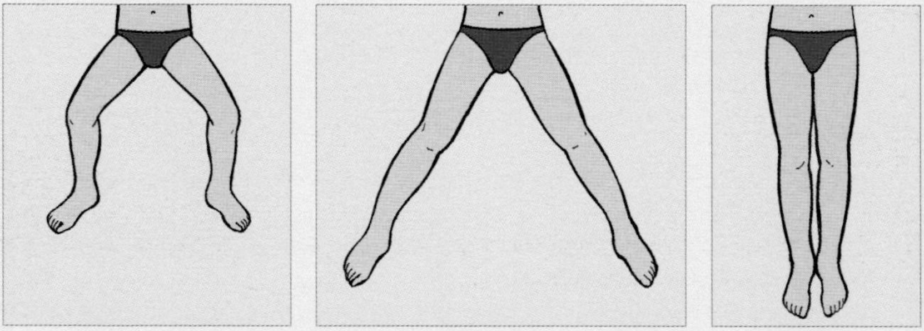

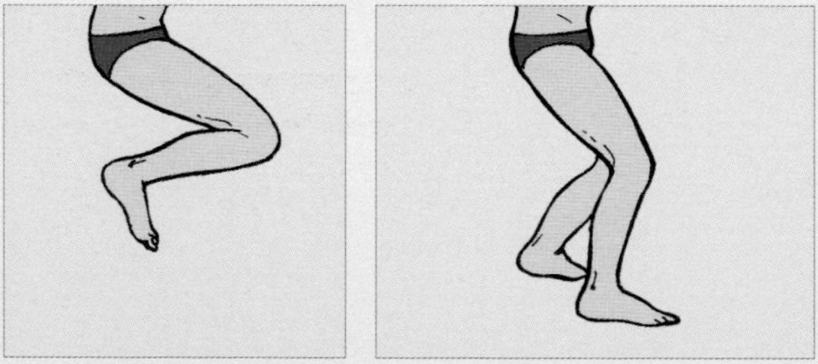

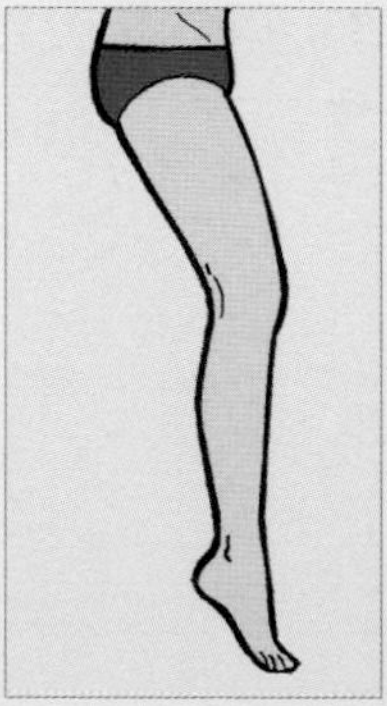

Leg action is a gentle, steady breaststroke kick. Some swimmers prefer the same kick with alternating legs.

HELP (heat escape lessening posture) position

If you are a long distance from the shore, you have a greater chance of survival if you stay motionless to conserve energy. Wait for help to arrive, and float using a life jacket or any other buoyancy device available.

If you are using a life jacket, keep your legs together, with your hands hooked into the collar of the life jacket and your elbows close into your sides. Let your legs drift into a natural position (it has been found that with progressive shivering and the general increase in muscle tension, people's hips take up this position automatically).

If no life jacket is available, use any floating object that will help you to rest in a position like the one described above.

The huddle

A small group of people can reduce the amount of heat they lose by huddling together. This is more effective if all members of the group are wearing life jackets.

The huddle is formed by each person allowing their legs to reach a comfortable, natural position, while placing their arms around the waist of those on either side. The positions of the legs should be adjusted to allow the group to become as stable as possible.

When life jackets are not being worn, the huddle position can be improvised by using any large floating object to support the group.

> If you are afloat in choppy water, it's a good idea to try to make sure your back is to the oncoming waves.

COMPETITIVE SWIMMING

Most people learn to swim as a way of keeping fit, as a fun thing to do with their leisure time, for safety reasons, or so that they can take part in water sports such as canoeing, sub-aqua, sailing or windsurfing. Many of us learn to swim at school.

Once they have learned the basics, some people find they have a particular natural ability at swimming. These are often the people who are attracted to competitive swimming. If this describes you, remember: being a racer is not an easy option! Great dedication, self-discipline and motivation are needed to reach high levels of performance.

Requirements

Anyone wanting to become a competitive swimmer will need the following:

- a practical knowledge of swimming skills, stroke techniques and methods of training

- physical fitness: as well as skill and the right mental attitude, a swimmer needs strength, suppleness and endurance

- a determination and willingness to work hard (the reward is that the discipline of training will give lasting physical and mental benefits to swimmers who can manage it)

- a healthy lifestyle, with regular habits of eating, working and sleeping.

Training methods

Successful swimming coaches use a variety of methods to enable swimmers to realise their potential. Training always emphasises sound technical ability, the development of endurance through distance swimming, and strength and power (using speed work in the water as well as land conditioning). One of the principles of training is to gradually increase the workload as well as the number of repetitions of particular exercises.

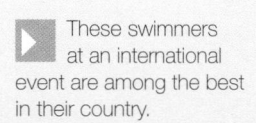 These swimmers at an international event are among the best in their country.

TYPICAL TRAINING

A typical training session for a competition swimmer might take the following form:

- warm-up swim to prepare muscles, heart and lungs for the more strenuous work to follow

- isolated practices (arms only; legs only) for strength and endurance, and to concentrate on aspects of technique

- full-stroke swimming – as fitness improves, distances and times can be varied and increased, with intervals set as required

- starts and turns practice – these can be of considerable advantage if performed well in competition, since they may make the difference between winning or losing a race

- warm-down swim, to allow the body to return to normal functioning.

LAND CONDITIONING

Although most training for swimming is done in the water, many swimmers also use some form of land conditioning. This helps them develop the strength, power, endurance and mobility needed to improve their level of fitness for competitive swimming. Such conditioning might include the following.

- Weight training – helps to develop strength, power and endurance.

- Pulley work – using special apparatus, the main muscle groups can be exercised.

- Circuit training – involves moving through a series of different exercises designed to increase strength and endurance.

- Mobility exercises – to increase the range of movements in the main joints.

- Energetic games – these add variety in addition to developing general physical fitness (sports used can include volleyball, squash, badminton and basketball).

JOINING A SWIMMING CLUB

At first, swimmers might prefer to practise and train alone. However, as they make progress, the time will come when expert advice and guidance is needed. This is the time to join a swimming club. Where there is a pool, there is usually a club too. Membership is comparatively inexpensive, and joining a club has many advantages:

- advice and guidance from qualified coaches and teachers

- working to specifically prepared training programmes

- working with others of equal ability

- the use of apparatus and equipment

- facilities for competition

- making new friends and enjoying social occasions with club members.

This young swimmer is racing at an age-group meet, against people of a similar age.

COMPETITIONS

There is a wide range of opportunities for competitive swimmers to race, ranging from local to international level.

- Internal swimming club events.

- Inter-club and league events.

- Open licensed and non-licensed meets.

- Age group competitions at ASA, county, regional and national level: these are divided by age group and include all four main strokes over distances from 50m, 100m, 200m, 400m, 800m and 1,500m for freestyle events, as well as medley events and relays.

- In addition to the National Age Group Championships, there are two main national events: (i) the short-course championships, taking place in 25-metre pools; and (ii) the long-course championships (also referred to as the National Championships) in 50-metre pools.

- English Schools National Championships, for school children only.

- Masters Competitions, which are open to swimmers aged 25 years and over.

GLOSSARY

Admission
Charge for spectators to watch competitive racing. Most events charge admission as a way of helping to pay for the cost of the pool.

Age group
Division of swimmers by age, for example under-10s, 11–12, 13–14, etc. Swimmers are also sometimes divided into Junior and Senior, and there are also Open meets, open to all ages.

Alternates
Sometimes also called 'reserves', these are the next-fastest two swimmers after those who have made it to the final of an event. If a qualifier drops out of the final, the alternative/reserve takes their place.

Anchor leg
The final leg in a relay race; the swimmer who swims it is sometimes called the 'anchor'.

Backstroke
One of the four competition strokes, swum on your back and with an alternating arm action.

Beep
The sound an electronic starting system makes to start the race.

Blocks
The starting platforms at either end of each lane, used for diving in and for gripping on to in a backstroke start.

Bottom
The underwater floor of the pool, which usually has lane marking on it to help the swimmers swim in a straight line.

Breaststroke
One of the four competition strokes, swum on your front and with both arms and legs making their kick together.

Butterfly
One of the four competition strokes, swum on your front and with both arms and legs making their kick together, and with an overarm recovery.

Camp
A get-together of swimmers for the purpose of coaching and training over a set period of time, usually either a whole weekend or a week. Many camps happen in the lead-up to a big meet.

Cap
The latex covering swimmers wear on their head, usually showing their team's colours.

Cards
Cards are handed out for each swimmer in a meet, and their times are recorded on them.

Check-in
Sometimes also called 'registration', this usually involves handing in your card for each of the events you are swimming. Check-in has to happen by a set time, which is usually shown on the card.

Consolation final

Sometimes also called the 'reserve final', this is a second final in which the 9th to 18th-fastest swimmers compete (if the competition is being held in an 8-lane pool).

Deck

The area around the pool reserved for swimmers, officials and coaches. No one else is allowed on deck during a competition.

Disqualified

Result not counted because one or more rules have been broken. Disqualifications (or 'DQ') are usually for a false start, or illegal turn, takeover or stroke technique.

Dive

Enter the water headfirst. Diving is sometimes not allowed in the warm-up except at set times.

Electronic timing

A highly accurate way of measuring the times swimmers do in each event. Most electronic timing systems are triggered by the starter's signal, and stopped by an electronic touch pad at the ends of each lane.

False-start rope

A rope across the entire width of the pool, which normally hangs in the air but is dropped into the water if there is a false start, as a way of stopping the swimmers.

FINA

Swimming's international governing body, which sets the sport's rules.

Finals

The deciding race in a championship meet. The fastest eight swimmers (if the pool has eight lanes) go into the final, the race that decides the ultimate winner.

Flags

A line of pennants that are hung across the whole width of the pool at each end, to warn backstroke racers that they are approaching a turn or finish.

Freestyle

One of the four competition strokes, swum on your front with alternating arm and legs actions and an overarm recovery.

Gallery

The viewing area for spectators.

Heats

Divisions of an event where there are too many swimmers simply to have a straight final. The fastest eight swimmers from the heats (if the event is in an eight-lane pool) go through to the final.

Individual medley

Often called simply 'IM', this is a race where one swimmer does each stroke in the following order: butterfly, backstroke, breaststroke, front crawl. Medley is also swum as a relay, in the order backstroke, breaststroke, butterfly, front crawl.

Kick

The leg action of a swimmer.

Kick board

A float used by swimmers who wish to practise their kicking action,

Long-course
Describes an event swum in a 50-metre pool.

Nationals
Shorthand for a country's national championships.

Open competition
A competition that any properly registered swimmer is allowed to enter.

Referee
The chief official at a swimming competition.

Relay
Swimming events in which four swimmers race as a team, one after the other. Relays are divided between medley relays (usually swum over 200 or 400 metres) and freestyle relays (usually swum over 200, 400 or 800 metres).

Scratch
To withdraw from an event at short notice, sometimes as a way of resting for another race, sometimes through injury or illness.

Seeding
The ranking of swimmers in an event according to times they have swum in the past.

Session
A portion of a competition, or a training session.

Shave-down
Removing all arm, leg and body hair as a way of decreasing drag. Only used by older swimmers at very important meets!

Short-course
Describes an event swum in a 25-metre pool.

Split
A time taken during the course of a race. For example, in a long-course 200-metre race the swimmer will record splits at 50 metres, 100 metres and 150 metres. Most top swimmers know exactly what splits they need to do to finish with a good time.

Stand up
The command given by the starter if he or she wants the swimmers to stand up from the starting position because of a problem.

Starter
The official in charge of signaling the start of the race.

Step down
The command given by the starter to ask the swimmers to step off the blocks, usually because there is some problem with the start.

Swim-off
A race to decide which of two swimmers with the same time will be included in the final.

Taper
The resting phase of training, where training becomes much lighter and more speed-orientated, as a big competition looms.

Touch out
Touch the wall ahead in a close race, often from a slightly behind position.

Touch pad
The pad that stops the electronic timing system.

Trials
A swimming competition held to decide who will be in the team for a particular event, such as the Olympics or World Championships.

Warm-down
The loosen-up swim after a hard training session or race.

Warm-up
The loosen-up swim before a training session or race.

Whistle
The whistle is used by the starter or referee to signal for quiet before a race is started.

Great Britain's Stacey Tadd gets ready to start the 400m individual medley at the 2005 European Junior Swimming Championships, Budapest.

SWIMMING WORLD AND OLYMPIC RECORDS

Listed below are the current world and Olympic record holders. To hold the world record is the ultimate achievement for any swimmer – quite simply, it means that no one on the planet has ever swum faster over that distance in competition.

The Olympics is the most prestigious stage for competition in the world. To hold the Olympic record takes not only great skill and fitness, but also mental strength to perform at the highest level.

MEN

50m Freestyle

Olympic – Alexander Popov, EUN, 21.91, 30 July 1992, Barcelona, Spain

World – Alexander Popov, RUS, 21.64, 16 June 2000, Moscow, Russia

100m Freestyle

Olympic – Pieter Van Den Hoogenband, NED, 47.84, 19 September 2000, Sydney, Australia

World – Pieter Van Den Hoogenband, NED, 47.84, 19 September 2000, Sydney, Australia

200m Freestyle

Olympic – Ian Thorpe, AUS, 1:44.71, 16 August 2004, Athens, Greece

World – Ian Thorpe, AUS, 1.44.06, 25 July 2001, Fukuoka, Japan

400m Freestyle

Olympic – Ian Thorpe, AUS, 3:40.59, 16 September 2000, Sydney, Australia

World – Ian Thorpe, AUS, 3:40.08, 30 July 2002, Manchester, England

1500m Freestyle

Olympic – Grant Hackett, AUS, 14:43.40, 21 August 2004, Athens, Greece

World – Grant Hackett, AUS, 14:34.56, 29 July 2001, Fukuoka, Japan

100m Backstroke

Olympic – Aaron Peirsol, USA, 53.45, 21 August 2004, Athens, Greece

World – Aaron Peirsol, USA, 53.17, 2 April 2005, Indianapolis, USA

200m Backstroke

Olympic – Aaron Peirsol, USA, 1:54.95, 19 August 2004, Athens, Greece

World – Aaron Peirsol, USA, 1:54.66, 29 July 2005, Montreal, Canada

100m Breaststroke

Olympic – Brendan Hansen, USA, 1:00.01, 14 August 2004, Athens, Greece

World – Brendan Hansen, USA, 59.30, 8 July 2004, Long Beach, USA

200m Breaststroke

Olympic – Kosuke Kitajima, JPN, 2:09.44, 18 August 2004, Athens, Greece

World – Brendan Hansen, USA, 2:09.04, 11 July 2004, Long Beach, USA

100m Butterfly

Olympic – Michael Phelps, USA, 51.25, 20 August 2004, Athens, Greece

World – Ian Crocker, USA, 50.40, 30 July 2005, Montreal, Canada

200m Butterfly

Olympic – Michael Phelps, USA, 1:54.04, 17 August 2004, Athens, Greece

World – Michael Phelps, USA, 1:53.93, 22 July 2003, Barcelona, Spain

200m Individual Medley

Olympic – Michael Phelps, USA, 1:57.14, 19 August 2004, Athens, Greece

World – Michael Phelps, USA, 1:55.94, 9 August 2003, College Park, USA

400m Individual Medley

Olympic – Michael Phelps, USA, 4:08.26, 14 August 2004, Athens, Greece

World – Michael Phelps, USA, 4:08.26, 14 August 2004, Athens, Greece

4x100m Freestyle Team Relay

Olympic – Roland Schoeman, Lyndon Ferns, Darian Townsend, Ryk Neethling, RSA, 3:13.17, 15 August 2004, Athens, Greece

World – Roland Schoeman, Lyndon Ferns, Darian Townsend, Ryk Neethling, RSA, 3:13.17, 15 August 2004, Athens, Greece

4x200m Freestyle Team Relay

Olympic – Ian Thorpe, Michael Klim, Todd Pearson, Bill Kirby, AUS, 7:07.05, 19 September 2000, Sydney, Australia

World – Grant Hackett, Michael Klim, Bill Kirby, Ian Thorpe, AUS, 7:04.66, 27 July 2001, Fukuoka, Japan

4x100m Medley Team Relay

Olympic – Aaron Peirsol, Brendan Hansen, Ian Crocker, Jason Lezak, USA, 3:30.68, 21 August 2004, Athens, Greece

World – Aaron Peirsol, Brendan Hansen, Ian Crocker, Jason Lezak, USA, 3:30.68, 21 August 2004, Athens, Greece

WOMEN

50m Freestyle

Olympic – Inge de Bruijn, NED, 24.13, 22 September 2000, Sydney, Australia

World – Inge de Bruijn, NED, 24.13, 22 September 2000, Sydney, Australia

100m Freestyle

Olympic – Jodie Henry, AUS, 53.52, 18 August 2004, Athens, Greece

World –Lisbeth Lenton, AUS, 53.42, 31 January 2006, Melbourne, Australia

200m Freestyle

Olympic – Heike Friedrich, GDR, 1:57.65, 21 September 1988, Seoul, Korea

World –Franziska Van Almsick, GER, 1:56.64, 3 August 2004, Berlin, Germany

400m Freestyle

Olympic – Janet Evans, USA, 4:03.85, 22 September 1988, Seoul, Korea

World – Janet Evans, USA, 4:03.85, 22 September 1988, Seoul, Korea

800m Freestyle

Olympic – Brooke Bennett, USA, 8:19.67, 22 September 2000, Sydney, Australia

World – Janet Evans, USA, 8:16.22, 20 August 1989, Tokyo, Japan

100m Backstroke

Olympic – Natalie Coughlin, USA, 59.68, 21 August 2004, Athens, Greece

World – Natalie Coughlin, USA, 59.58, 13 August 2002, Fort Lauderdale, USA

200m Backstroke

Olympic – Krisztina Egerszegi, HUN, 2:07.06, 31 July 1992, Barcelona, Spain

World – Krisztina Egerszegi, HUN, 2:06.62, 25 August 1991, Athens, Greece

100m Breaststroke

Olympic – Xuejuan Luo, CHN, 1:06.64, 16 August 2004, Athens, Greece

World – Leisel Jones, AUS, 1:05.09, 20 March 2006, Melbourne, Australia

200m Breaststroke

Olympic – Amanda Beard, USA, 2:23.37, 19 August 2004, Athens, Greece

World – Leisel Jones, AUS, 2:20.54, 1 February 2006, Melbourne, Australia

100m Butterfly

Olympic – Inge de Bruijn, NED, 56.61, 17 September 2000, Sydney, Australia

World – Inge de Bruijn, NED, 56.61, 17 September 2000, Sydney, Australia

200m Butterfly

Olympic – Misty Hyman, USA, 2:05.88, 20 September 2000, Sydney, Australia

World – Otylia Jedrzejczak, POL, 2:05.61, 28 July 2005, Montreal, Canada

200m Individual Medley

Olympic – Yana Klochova, UKR, 2:10.68, 19 September 2000, Sydney, Australia

World – Yanyan Wu, CHN, 2:09.72, 17 October 1997, Shanghai, China

400m Individual Medley

Olympic – Yana Klochova, UKR, 4:33.59, 16 September 2000, Sydney, Australia

World – Yana Klochova, UKR, 4:33.59, 16 September 2000, Sydney, Australia

4x100m Freestyle Team Relay

Olympic – Alice Mills, Lisbeth Lenton, Petria Thomas, Jodie Henry, AUS, 3:35.94, 14 August 2000, Sydney, Australia

World – Alice Mills, Lisbeth Lenton, Petria Thomas, Jodie Henry, AUS, 3:35.94, 14 August 2000, Sydney, Australia

4x200m Freestyle Team Relay

Olympic – Natalie Coughlin, Carly Piper, Dana Vollmer, Kaitlin Sandeno, USA, 7:53.42, 18 August 2004, Athens, Greece

World – Natalie Coughlin, Carly Piper, Dana Vollmer, Kaitlin Sandeno, USA, 7:53.42, 18 August 2004, Athens, Greece

4x100m Medley Team Relay

Olympic – Giaan Rooney, Leisel Jones, Petria Thomas, Jodie Henry, AUS, 3:57.32, 21 August 2004, Athens, Greece

World – Sophie Edington, Leisel Jones, Jess Schipper, Lisbeth Lenton, AUS, 3:56.30, 21 March 2006, Melbourne, Australia

Michael Phelps on his way to the Olympic record in the 200m butterfly in Athens, 2004.

INDEX